Seeds of Knowledge

PREVIOUSLY PUBLISHED WITH RESOURCE PUBLICATIONS

Nonfiction

Storms Are Faith's Workout: Preparing Christians for Spiritual Ambush (2018).
Faith's Journey Confronts Obstacles: Instructing God's Soldiers to Overcome in His Armor (2019).
Satan's Strategy to Torment Through Physical Ambush: Educating God's Soldiers of Satan's Plot to Shatter Faith through Sickness and Disease (2019).
Spiritual Shipwreck on the Horizon: Exhorting Christians to Contend for the Faith and Comprehend the Deceitfulness of Sin (2019).
Satan Has No Authority Over God's Soldier: Illuminating Godlike Faith (2019).
God: The Holy Spirit: The Conquering Power Within (2019).
Signs of the Time: Warning: Lukewarm Christianity Accepts Deception (2020)
Flesh and Spirit Conflict: The Inner Battle of Choice (2020).
Supernatural Faith Disables: Quench the Fiery Darts (2020).

Fiction

The Elfdins and the Gold Temple: An Oralee Chronicle (2018).
Charlie McGee and the Leprechaun: Life's Curious Twist of Events (2019).
The Shrines of Manitoba: Dark Secrets Shall Be Brought to Light (2019).
Guilty As Blood: One Can Make a Difference (2019).
Back From the Dead: Light Shines As the Noonday Sun (2020).
Nazis, Holocaust, and Self-Love: Unbridled Bigotry (2020).
Chateau de Paix: Nightmare Hiding In Paradise (2020).

Seeds of Knowledge

Soil Determines the Seed's Harvest

R. C. JETTE

RESOURCE *Publications* • Eugene, Oregon

SEEDS OF KNOWLEDGE
Soil Determines the Seed's Harvest

Copyright © 2020 R. C. Jette. All rights reserved. Except for brief quotations in critical publications or reviews, no part of this book may be reproduced in any manner without prior written permission from the publisher. Write: Permissions, Wipf and Stock Publishers, 199 W. 8th Ave., Suite 3, Eugene, OR 97401.

All Scripture references are taken from the KING JAMES VERSION (KJV): KING JAMES VERSION, public domain.

Resource Publications
An Imprint of Wipf and Stock Publishers
199 W. 8th Ave., Suite 3
Eugene, OR 97401

www.wipfandstock.com

PAPERBACK ISBN: 978-1-7252-8880-5
HARDCOVER ISBN: 978-1-7252-8881-2
EBOOK ISBN: 978-1-7252-8882-9

Manufactured in the U.S.A.   12/07/20

This book is dedicated to my Lord Jesus Christ
who makes the impossible possible by faith.
To my husband (Paul) who has been
by my side through thick and thin.
My son (PJ) his daughter (Kierra). My daughter (Dawn) who
has freed me up to write. My daughter (Christina) her sons
(Andrew, Matthew, Joshua) and her daughter (Sarah) who is
with the Lord. My father-in-law (Albert) who is with the Lord.
Also, my mother (Rita Christina), my brothers (Frank and
Raymond), my sister (Carol), and other family and relatives
awaiting the grand reunion day.
Susanna and Mike who have been such a help,
and to all who have influenced my life throughout the years.
My special thanks is given to Wipf and Stock Publishers for
their continued publication of my books under their Resource
Publications. I am grateful to Joe Delahanty, Jim Tedrick,
Zechariah Mickel, Ian Creeger, Stephanie Randels.
Special mention is given to Matthew Wimer, George Callihan,
Shannon Carter, and Savanah N. Landerholm to whom words
cannot convey my gratitude.

Who shall separate us from the love of Christ? shall tribulation, or distress, or persecution, or famine, or nakedness, or peril, or sword? As it is written, For thy sake we are killed all the day long; we are accounted as sheep for the slaughter. Nay, in all these things we are more than conquerors through him that loved us. For I am persuaded, that neither death, nor life, nor angels, nor principalities, nor powers, nor things present, nor things to come, Nor height, nor depth, nor any other creature, shall be able to separate us from the love of God, which is in Christ Jesus our Lord.

—Romans 8:35–39.

Thy word is a lamp unto my feet, and a light unto my path.

—Psalm 119:105.

Contents

Introduction		ix
Chapter 1	Seeds Flourish In Good Soil	1
Chapter 2	Good Soil Endures Affliction	10
Chapter 3	God's Love Is Key To Good Soil	18
Chapter 4	God Cannot Be Compared	34
Chapter 5	Belief In God's Word Determines Soil	41
Chapter 6	God's Soldiers Are Upheld	48
Chapter 7	Good Soil Brings Forth His Craftsmanship	55

Introduction

SOMETIMES WE THINK THE darkness (storm, trial, obstacle, sin, situation, etc.) in our life is unconquerable and unsurmountable. It is as if there is no end in sight, and we feel as if we are fighting a losing battle. However, the problem is not the dilemma we have found ourselves in, it's our lack of preparation before the sudden darkness. If we had been properly equipped, we would not be bombarded by questions of doubt or unbelief or instigated by the scoffers or the ridiculers. Proper planning would have us walking in his light and standing by faith no matter how dark the situation, no matter how severe the storm, no matter how huge the obstacle, or how diabolical Satan's strategy.

This book is meant to reveal why so many of God's soldiers are ill prepared for the darkness that tries to assail us daily and are becoming victims during the storms instead of being the victors. It is all based on the ground/soil the seeds of knowledge, the promises, the revelations are sown into that determines what is done during the darkness/storm/obstacle/ strategy and the results of our harvest.

If we forget that we fight daily against an unrelenting enemy out to destroy us and our faith, we will be overwhelmed by the darkness. The seeds of knowledge will fall upon fallow or neglected ground and be disabled. Only the light of God's word will light our path through the darkness of trials to victory.

As with all my nonfiction books, each chapter is meant to build on the previous chapter to illuminate the whole. An understanding of what is done each time a seed of knowledge, a promise, or a revelation is sown, will help us to comprehend the importance

INTRODUCTION

of studying God's word. I will bring forth the importance of tending the seeds of knowledge by revealing various seeds sown in our life and what is done with the word of God once sown.

Only as we realize the importance of the light of God's word, will we be enabled to face any darkness that the devil hurls at us. Without the light, we will stumble around in the darkness until we are consumed by its power. The more we nurture the seed of God's word, the more knowledge is received. The more knowledge yields more light and more light produces a greater harvest of fruit.

At present, it seems the darkness (storms, obstacles, trials, sin, situations, etc.) is trying to consume many of God's soldiers. If you are one of those trying to overcome an incredible hurdle in your life, the Lord has led you to this book to gain the knowledge you need to face this darkness. You cannot do it alone. Only Jesus, who is the word made flesh, can give you the light of his word needed to see your way through this heavy shroud. Don't despair, but read through to the end and grasp hold of what you need to do in your life to walk in God's light, receive a harvest of fruit, and overcome any darkness you may face!

Chapter 1

Seeds Flourish In Good Soil

Hearken; Behold, there went out a sower to sow: And it came to pass, as he sowed, some fell by the way side, and the fowls of the air came and devoured it up. And some fell on stony ground, where it had not much earth; and immediately it sprang up, because it had no depth of earth: But when the sun was up, it was scorched; and because it had no root, it withered away. And some fell among thorns, and the thorns grew up, and choked it, and it yielded no fruit. And other fell on good ground, and did yield fruit that sprang up and increased; and brought forth, some thirty, and some sixty, and some an hundred. And he said unto them, He that hath ears to hear, let him hear (Mark 4:3–9).

ALTHOUGH THESE SCRIPTURES ARE the usual to reveal the types of ground or soil the sower sows his seed to bring forth salvation, for this book, it is to reveal the ground upon which the word of God, the seed of knowledge, a promise, or a revelation is sown.

Each type of ground listed in Luke 8:5–8 will be illuminated to disclose why some Christians seem to grow in our faith walk and others do not. It is imperative to understand the soil in which the seeds are sown is the condition of our heart at any given moment.

With that knowledge, we will be enabled to realize why sometimes we aren't growing in knowledge and understanding of God's word, and we will receive insight as to why we sometimes miss out on the promises of God.

Jesus used four different types of ground or soils in which the seeds are sown. For this book, it is meant to reveal to God's soldiers the different conditions, environments, atmospheres, and circumstances that effect our heart when the seed is sown. What is transpiring in our heart at the time of the sowing? Whatever happens to the seed sown is determined by that factor. The condition of the soil or ground upon which the seeds of knowledge fall are continuous. What I mean, is that at any moment, we can allow our heart to reject the seed of God's word. This will be made clear as we go along in this book.

At this time, let's begin to unfold the types of ground upon which God's word, the seed of knowledge, a promise, or a revelation is sown in our heart. Is it the wayside, stony ground, thorns, or good ground?

SEED SOWN BY THE WAYSIDE

> And these are they by the way side, where the word is sown; but when they have heard, Satan cometh immediately, and taketh away the word that was sown in their hearts (Mark 4:15).

When the seed is sown in this heart, it is immediately snatched away by the devil. How can the devil immediately snatch away the seed the Lord plants? There is no handicap, infirmity, impediment, restriction, etc. in the seed or in his word.

> So shall my word be that goeth forth out of my mouth: it shall not return unto me void, but it shall accomplish that which I please, and it shall prosper in the thing whereto I sent it (Isaiah 55:11).

God's word is capable of performing whatever He has sent it to do, for the power and effect of God's word will never be rescinded or become void.

Since God's word is efficacious, how was Satan able to seize the seed as quickly as it was sown? The answer is simple. The heart in which it was sown rejected the word of God, the seed of knowledge, a promise, or a revelation. It was not believed, and our heart refused to listen to it.

We either thought it was not important for us to learn and rejected it, or we believed the promise was impossible, or we would not deny self to receive it. Whatever the reason that enabled Satan to take hold of the seed was not any liability of the word.

Let me explain how this can happen. We read these verses: "For if ye forgive men their trespasses, your heavenly Father will also forgive you: But if ye forgive not men their trespasses, neither will your Father forgive your trespasses" (Matthew 6:14–15). If we decide there is no way God expects me to forgive him or her for what was done, we reject its truth and ignore the word sown. Immediately the devil snatches that seed of knowledge and we remain in the sin of unforgiveness. Furthermore, we lose the promise of being forgiven by the Lord for our sins.

The seed sown by the wayside is a heart that is not prepared to receive God's truth no matter how uncomfortable on our flesh. We have not learned to deny self and we choose to reject or ignore the seed of knowledge we read or hear. Thus, instead of walking in the light of God's word, we remain in the darkness of deceit.

If we look around, we can name Christians who are living in some sin because of a refusal to obey the truth of God's word. As soon as it was sown, Satan came and snatched it up because we dismissed its truth. The devil has convinced us through false teachers that we can continue in sin and still go to heaven. Yet, the word makes clear that those doing such will not inherit the kingdom of God.

Seeds of Knowledge

SEED SOWN ON STONY GROUND

> And these are they likewise which are sown on stony ground; who, when they have heard the word, immediately receive it with gladness; And have no root in themselves, and so endure but for a time: afterward, when affliction or persecution ariseth for the word's sake, immediately they are offended (Mark 4:16–17).

It's obvious this heart liked what it hears, for the word of God is immediately received with gladness. This is the soil that accepts what it hears or reads, but is not willing to deny self to endure the heat of the day.

When the heat of persecution, ridicule, harassment, etc. comes, we are not willing to deny self. We have no depth of consecration. Christ is not our life; we are. We do not love God with all our heart, all our soul, all our mind, and all our strength (Mark 12:30). For a clearer understanding of our love for God and his love for us, please read my book, *Storms Are Faith's Workout: Preparing Christians for Spiritual Ambush.*

Without a comprehension of God's love, there is no root to endure, no stability to stand against the trial, storm, obstacle, strategy, etc. of the devil. Our love of God was contingent upon everything going along fine without hurdles. We do not like ripples in our life, so we are offended, affronted, insulted, hurt, etc. when things get tough.

> Yea, and all that will live godly in Christ Jesus shall suffer persecution (2 Timothy 3:12).

Let's face it, this is seen daily in Christians who back down from biblical truths because we do not want to suffer or endure persecution, harassment, affliction for the sake of God's kingdom. We do not want to lose friends. We do not want to be called names or accused of hating for our faith. We are no longer willing to live a godly life, for we cannot endure the persecution.

Because many of us have become spineless, cowardly, gutless, or fainthearted, things have become out of control in our country. Satan and his cohorts have infiltrated every aspect of America to destroy it, and the church has been sitting on the sidelines watching the sky.

Yes, we are to be aware of Christ's second coming, but not sit idly by while our country is being overtaken by evil. The escapism mentality will not bind the powers of Hell. For more about this truth, please read, *Signs Of the Time: Warning: Lukewarm Christianity Accepts Deception*.

We are to occupy, dominate, conquer, etc. until Christ returns (Luke 19:13). Looking for a way out of everything is not occupying. It is not standing against the wiles of the devil. It is not pushing back the gates of Hell trying to destroy the church and our One Nation Under God.

> Whosoever therefore shall confess me before men, him will I confess also before my Father which is in heaven. But whosoever shall deny me before men, him will I also deny before my Father which is in heaven (Matthew 10:32-33).

When we are offended for the word's sake, we have chosen to deny Christ before those we are committing spiritual adultery with. It's not just the matter of allowing our heart to be hardened by the persecution or the affliction, but the eternal consequences that result.

When we are offended and refuse to stand against the persecution for Christ, we are allowing the seeds of knowledge or God's word to fall on stony ground. We are refusing to suffer persecution for Christ's sake. We are denying Christ because we do not want the harassment for the truth of God's word. We refuse to endure the heat of persecution and our faith withers.

Although that is quite sobering, have we considered the seriousness of that decision? Because we do not want the harassment, we are denying Christ before men. To deny him here means He will deny us before his Father in heaven (Matthew 10:33).

SEED SOWN AMONG THORNS

> And these are they which are sown among thorns; such as hear the word, And the cares of this world; and the deceitfulness of riches, and the lusts of other things entering in, choke the word, and it becometh unfruitful (Mark 4:18-19).

Seeds of Knowledge

> And the Lord said unto Moses, Depart, and go up hence, thou and the people which thou hast brought up out of the land of Egypt, unto the land which I sware unto Abraham, to Isaac, and to Jacob, saying, Unto thy seed will I give it: And I will send an angel before thee, and I will drive out the Canaanite the Amorite and the Hittite and the Perizzite the Hivite and the Jebusite: Unto a land flowing with milk and honey. . .(Exodus 33:1-3).

In the verses in Exodus, God promises to drive out the inhabitants of the Promise Land or the land flowing with milk and honey. Yet, in Numbers chapters 13-14, after the twelve spies come back claiming it was truly a land flowing with milk and honey, ten spies give an evil report.

Let us understand how the Israelites believed the ten spies with the evil report. First, we have to ask how can thorns choke the word? How can thorns choke the life out of the word? What are thorns according to the parable in Mark?

Thorns are the cares of this world, the deceitfulness of riches, and the lusts of other things entering in. When they get hold of a heart, they choke the life out of the word sown.

The Israelites love of self or their life is a lusts of other things that choked the word of God given them. They feared so much for their life that they forgot God had promised to send his angel before them to drive out the inhabitants. God's word was choked by the lusts of fear for their life.

> Perverse disputings of men of corrupt minds, and destitute of the truth, supposing that gain is godliness: from such withdraw thyself. But godliness with contentment is great gain. For we brought nothing into this world, and it is certain we can carry nothing out. And having food and raiment let us be therewith content. But they that will be rich fall into temptation and a snare, and into many foolish and hurtful lusts, which drown men in destruction and perdition. For the love of money is the root of all evil: which while some coveted after, they have erred from the faith, and pierced themselves through with many sorrows (1 Timothy 6:5-10).

The sad thing is that many Christians are seeking after money. We are focused on how to get more money. We are deceived into believing money will bring happiness. When we are obsessed with having more money, we have become destitute or robbed of the truth into believing that financial gain proves God's favor. That mentality was the prominent belief in Job's day. So, when he was in his storm, his friends accused him of being some great sinner.

Gain or wealth is not the sign of godliness. How many wealthy are living unrighteous and ungodly lives according to scripture? How many are living lives according to the false teaches of gain is godliness while living in sin? I am not saying God will not bless his children. I am saying when He does, righteousness, godliness, and holiness, according to his word, will be evident in our life. Our life will be opposite of those who live according to the world's standard. We will resemble Christ in our life.

> Be careful for nothing; but in every thing by prayer and supplication with thanksgiving let your requests be made known unto God. And the peace of God, which passeth all understanding, shall keep your hearts and minds through Christ Jesus (Philippians 4:6–7).

When we are careful or anxious, we have become self-centered. We have allowed the cares of this world to consume us. We seem to be worried about everything and anything. How many times have we seen Christians steadfast in their walk, and then see them walk back into the world?

As we entertain worry or anxiety, it will be self-destructive to our faith. The promises of God are choked by the thorns. When promises are choked, we forget that He will supply all our need according to his riches in glory by Christ Jesus (Philippians 4:19); we forget if we seek first the kingdom of God, and his righteousness that all these things shall be added unto us (Matthew 6:33); we forget that we can do all things through Christ which strengtheneth us (Philippians 4:13).

It's imperative to realize the thorns of the cares of this world, the deceitfulness of riches, and the lusts of other things will choke all the promises of God. Whatever promise of God's word had been sown will be strangled and we will become unfruitful. We will not harvest any of the knowledge or promises sown. In fact, our faith in God is choked or strangled and unbelief is harvested instead of faith.

SEED SOWN ON GOOD GROUND

> And these are they which are sown on good ground: such as hear the word, and receive it, and bring forth fruit, some thirty-fold, some sixty, and some an hundred (Mark 4:20).

When the seed is sown on good ground or soil prepared to receive it, it will harvest God's intention for the word in our life.

> And he said to them all, If any man will come after me, let him deny himself, and take up his cross daily, and follow me. (Luke 9:23).

If Jesus is our Lord and Savior, we have chosen to believe God's word, have committed ourselves to follow him no matter the cost. This requires a daily self-denial and a willingness to ignore what we want and choose his will.

To take up our cross daily is to expect distressing situations each day because of our fidelity to Christ. Too many Christians are not preparing themselves for daily hardships and when things get tough, we are either the wayside of rejecting God's word, the stony ground that can't take the heat of persecution, or we allow the thorns to choke the word because of the cares of this world, the deceitfulness of riches, or the lusts of other things (lust of the flesh, lust of the eyes, or the pride of life).

How does the good ground prepare itself to receive the seed of God's word. It chooses to live for Christ, deny self, and take up our heavy cross daily. This is not a once and for all decision; it is made continuously, repeatedly, without wavering. Our choice to deny self determines the fruit or harvest we reap.

Some of us will reap knowledge thirty-fold, others sixty, and others will reap an hundred. I believe our course in life will determine the extent of our knowledge. However, it will always be what we need to live victoriously in Christ,

What do I mean by that? Well, a minister of the gospel will definitely need more knowledge to feed the sheep. A parent will need a certain amount to train his/her child in the way to go. Simply put, if we have been planting the seed of God's word in good soil, we will have sufficient knowledge to accomplish whatever is needed.

Having sufficient knowledge will enable us to overcome whatever Satan hurls at us, and we will receive every promise God has *sown* in our heart.

This chapter is meant to enlighten God's soldiers to various soils into which the seed of knowledge or God's word is sown. Unless we have chosen to love the Lord our God with all our heart, with all our soul, with all our strength, and with all our mind (Luke 10:27), have chosen to deny ourselves, take up our cross daily, and follow him (Luke 9:23), and have chosen to believe He loves us (Romans 5:8), we are not preparing our soil to be good ground.

Have we permitted the cares of the world, the deceitfulness of riches, and the lusts of other things to choke the word and miss God's promise? Have we permitted our heart to receive the words of false teachers, scoffers, gainsayers, etc.?

God's word is efficacious. It is able to perform what He ordained it to do. When it does not, it is due to the soil it was sown in. Our heart is the soil. What is the condition of our heart at the time of the sown word? Have we decided to reject it because we do not like what it says? Have we allowed persecution or affliction because of the word to cause us to deny Christ?

Our harvest is determined by the soil the seed is sown in. We are the ones who either prepare our soil to reject the seed, deny Christ, be overcome by this world and its lusts, and bring forth no fruit. Whereas, if we deny self, love God with our whole being, believe He loves us, we will bring forth fruit thirty-fold, sixty, or an hundred!

Chapter 2

Good Soil Endures Affliction

Thou therefore endure hardness, as a good soldier of Jesus Christ. No man that warreth entangleth himself with the affairs of this life; that he may please him who hath chosen him to be a soldier. And if a man also strive for masteries, yet is he not crowned, except he strive lawfully. The husbandman that laboureth must be first partaker of the fruits. Consider what I say; and the Lord give thee understanding in all things (2 Timothy 2:3–7).

IF GOD'S SOLDIERS ARE to endure or overcome, we must be single-minded in our endeavor to please God. As we remain faithful to Christ, we will encounter adversity and resistance. In simple terms, following Christ is not a tip-toe through the tulips. It means clothing ourselves in the full armor of God and realizing our life is now one of continuous combat. For more about this truth, please read my book, *Faith's Journey Confronts Obstacles: Instructing God's Soldiers to Overcome in His Armor*.

When we enlisted in the Army of the Lord, we signed up for a lifetime of warfare against a relentless enemy who wants us destroyed. We do not wrestle or fight against flesh and blood, but against principalities, against powers, against the rulers of the darkness of this world, against spiritual wickedness in high places (Ephesians 6:12).

To help us understand what is meant by enduring hardness or affliction, the Apostle gives three examples of endurance: the soldier, the athlete, and the farmer.

THE SOLDIER

A soldier, who desires to please his commanding officer, must be willing to face fierce opposition and experience suffering. God's soldiers must be willing to endure hardness as we wage spiritual warfare against the powers of Hell. Our fidelity to Christ must be so committed that we will stand in the whole armor of God and fight against the gates of Hell trying to destroy us, our loved ones, our country, etc.

> For which of you, intending to build a tower, sitteth not down first, and counteth the cost, whether he have sufficient to finish it? Lest haply, after he hath laid the foundation, and is not able to finish it, all that behold it begin to mock him, Saying, This man began to build, and was not able to finish (Luke 14:28–30).

When we join the army of God, we have to consider the cost before making the commitment. Too many are beguiled into thinking that all their troubles or trials end when accepting Christ as Savior. Too many are beguiled into thinking that a simple prayer means they can continue in sin and still go to heaven. Too many are beguiled into thinking that godliness is gain or that wealth is the sign of godliness.

Paul is revealing the absurdity of those who undertook to be disciples of Christ without considering the hardships or difficulties that we will meet with and the strength and endurance needed to continue.

> And he said to them, If any man will come after me, let him deny himself, and take up his cross daily, and follow me (Luke 9:23).

Without comprehending the COST of being a soldier is self-denial, our steadfastness to Christ will either be snatched by the devil, be destroyed by the heat of persecution, or be choked by the cares of this world, the deceitfulness of riches, or other lusts entering in.

If we are to build our tower or endure the opposition of being God's soldier, we must learn and practice self-denial. It will cost us the denial of what we want, desire, etc. and choose his will. This choice will always be uncomfortable on our flesh. Our flesh will never choose what makes it uncomfortable, what squeezes it, or what denies it.

> Enter ye in at the strait gate: for wide is the gate, and broad is the way, that leadeth to destruction, and many there be which go in thereat: Because strait is the gate, and narrow is the way, which leadeth unto life, and few there be that find it (Matthew 7:13–14).

This a sobering statement by Christ. He is teaching his soldiers that we shouldn't expect a multitude to follow on the road that leads to eternal life, and it can be a lonely journey. We must comprehend the fact that not many will be willing to inconvenience our flesh. We are easily enticed by the pleasures of the world around us. We believe we can have one foot in God's kingdom and one foot in the world. However, Christ makes clear that those who refuse to be either hot or cold and insist upon being lukewarm, He will spue out of his mouth (Revelation 3:16).

As a matter of fact, few will pass through the gate of godly humility and true repentance that is required to enter eternal life. Only those of us who have repented from going our own way and are willing to follow Jesus on this difficult and arduous voyage of self-denial will be the FEW who enter into the straight and narrow gate that leads to life.

God's soldiers must be willing to endure hardness, persecution, affliction, hostility, etc. for the sake of Christ if we are to enter into eternal life. This means living a life with one goal and one goal only and that is to please him who has chosen us to be his soldier.

THE ATHLETE

As an athlete who disciplines self to achieve the end results, God's soldiers must live a life of self-discipline and choose to sacrifice fleshly comforts to accomplish the end results.

> Know ye not that they which run in a race run all, but one receiveth the prize? So run, that ye may obtain. And every man that striveth for the mastery is temperate in all things. Now they do it to obtain a corruptible crown; but we an incorruptible. I therefore so run, not as uncertainly; so fight I, not as one that beateth the air: But I keep under my body, and bring it into subjection: lets that by any means, when I have preached to others, I myself should be a castaway (1 Corinthians 9:24-27).

We must be as earnest to attain Heaven as men are to win a race or wrestle an opponent. Athletes, to accomplish their goal of winning their contest, must endure years of severe training with severe self-discipline. If we are to win or overcome this life, we must be persistent and practice self-restraint.

When we think about athletes, we are reminded of the Olympic athletes who are some of the toughest people we know. These people do not just love the sport they compete in, but it is their life. Most of their life is devoted to their goal of winning an Olympic medal.

Many of these athletes spend four to eight years training in a sport before they make an Olympic team. They do not take lightly their endeavor and plan training schedules years in advance in order to work towards and accomplish their specific goals.

While their friends may be out socializing, the Olympic athletes are denying their flesh any recreation that could hinder their goal of winning the medal. They make sure they adhere to a strict diet, get the sleep needed, and keep themselves in the right state of mind in order to stay on top of their game.

Once God's soldiers recognize we are spiritual athletes, it should change our outlook on how we live our life. We should be totally transformed in our thinking, our goals, and our life in general.

Paul in the scriptures in 1 Corinthians is teaching us the world runs to win a corruptible crown that will fade away and rot. Even though the Olympic athletes are aware of this fact, the participants are temperate. They abstain from all that could be a hindrance to their winning the contest or the race. They train laboriously knowing that only one will win the gold.

Do God's soldiers comprehend our race is life threatening? Do we realize our spiritual well-being is at risk? Do we understand the importance of abstaining from whatever could hinder our winning or receiving our crown of life?

The Apostle Paul understood this reality and kept his body under and brought it into subjection to the will of God. He knew the dangers of becoming disheartened, dispirited, discouraged, depressed by the daily battles he encountered. He fully comprehended if he did not keep his fleshly appetites under control, he would be disqualified from winning his crown.

We must never stop being temperate in our desires, restrained in our flesh, and constant in our devotion to God. As God's soldier, we must always be self-restraining. Bridles are put into a horse's mouth to control its direction, we must bridle our wants/desires that are the opposite of God's will for our life. We must practice temperance or self-control daily if we are going to win the crown of life.

The rewarding thought is that not only one can win our crown. But all who run the race with temperance, that is characterized by moral and spiritual purity, integrity, separation from evil and complete dedication to God, will finish the race and win the prize of eternal life.

THE FARMER

The main goal of a farmer is to produce a good crop that is needed for survival. Without food, we would starve and eventually die. Farmers work hard to keep a supply of products for consumption. Farmers are necessary to keep a supply of essential foods for subsistence.

GOOD SOIL ENDURES AFFLICTION

Be patient therefore, brethren, unto the coming of the Lord. Behold, the husbandman waiteth for the precious fruit of the earth, and hath long patience for it, until he receive the early and latter rain (James 5:7).

As the farmer sows his seed, God's soldiers have sown our seed of deliverance from this world. Our harvest of whatever God has promised will take place, but it will take much patience, persistence, endurance to overcome the onslaught of adversities in our life.

The farmer must wait patiently for his crops to grow. There is no magical potion to plant one day and harvest the next. God's soldiers must learn to endure or persevere with all long-suffering if we are to harvest the crop God has sown in our heart.

In my book, *Spiritual Shipwreck on the Horizon: Exhorting Christians to Content for the Faith and Comprehend the Deceitfulness of Sin*, I explain the importance of temperance and the need for fidelity. Our devotion to Christ is the basis or foundation to our overcoming in this life. Without self-control, we will never persist, endure, or withstand the danger that can take place between seedtime and harvest. The storms, trials, obstacles, or strategy of Satan always come between seedtime and harvest. It is as certain as the sun rising and setting each day.

The most difficult time emerges after the sowing of the seed of God's word, promise, or revelation, and persists until the harvest. This is the time the enemy wages his vendetta to destroy our faith, our trust, our loyalty, and our love for God.

Let me keep building and explain a little more about seedtime and harvest. If we plant a crop or seed, we do not go out the next day or the next week and expect to harvest. We realize there is no magic charm or talisman to sow one day and harvest the next. We know we have to water, perhaps fertilize, keep out weeds, and shoo away any varmints. It takes time, sweat, and work to receive a harvest.

The same goes for the seed of a word, a promise, or a revelation planted by God. It is during this time between seedtime and harvest that our faith can be sorely tried. We have to be conscious of continuously feeding, watering, and fertilizing that seed with the word of God. Only God's word will give us light through the darkness of the storm.

Seeds of Knowledge

We have to constantly keep out weeds of doubt, fear, and questions. However, the most time-consuming effort can be shooing away the varmints who would try to encourage the weeds of doubt and questions. It is usually our family, our friends, our co-workers, etc. that plant seeds of doubt that question. Did God really say it? Will God really do it? Does God really want us to do this or to do that? We have all experienced the Genesis 3:1 crowd, *"Hath God said?"*

During the storms between seedtime and harvest is the test of what we believe. Do we really trust God's love for us? Do we really love him with all our heart, with all our soul, with all our strength, and with all our mind? Do we honestly believe his word?

Our fidelity will always be tested between seedtime and harvest. We can expect an attack to follow the sowing of the seed of God's word, promise, or revelation, and persist until the harvest. Any attack is meant to destroy our faith, our trust, our loyalty, and our love for God. If we understand that, we will not be ignorant of its intention. Only then can we stand against the violent assaults that want us destroyed, and declare as the husbandman or farmer that we will be partaker of our fruits.

Let me make clear the demonic attacks between seedtime and harvest can rage on for days, for weeks, for months, or for years. If we do not continuously feed the seed with God's word to grow strong in our knowledge of God, the seed will be snatched up by Satan, destroyed by the heat of persecution, or choked by the cares of this world, the deceitfulness of riches, or other lusts entering in.

The farmer comprehends his life is contingent upon his crop. God's soldiers must understand our spiritual life is contingent upon our harvest.

If we realize that once we have chosen to be a soldier of God, we have chosen a life of adversity, we will have our heart prepared for battle. We cannot fight today and decide to compromise tomorrow. Because the soldier is concerned about pleasing his superior officer, he does not entangle himself with the affairs of this life. God's soldiers must not concern ourselves with the affairs of this life but focus on pleasing him who has called us to be a soldier.

GOOD SOIL ENDURES AFFLICTION

The athlete does not practice self-restraint one day and indulge the next. He has one goal and that is to win his crown or prize. He is willing to suffer whatever inconvenience to his flesh that will enable him to run his best race. Once God's soldiers comprehend our crown carries eternal consequences, we will gladly deny self its lust of the flesh, lust of the eyes, and pride of life to win our eternal crown.

Farmers are steadfast in their effort to bring forth a good harvest. Their well-being is contingent upon the harvest. God's soldiers must learn the patience or long-suffering needed between seedtime and harvest.

As each seed of knowledge is sown, it will reveal the condition of our heart. Will the seed fall by the wayside, on stony ground, among thorns, or on good ground? If it is to be sown in good soil, it will take perseverance, tenacity, determination, dedication, etc. to bring forth a thirty-fold, sixty-fold, or an hundred-fold harvest of whatever God has promised!

Chapter 3

God's Love Is Key To Good Soil

> For when we were yet without strength, in due time Christ died for the ungodly. For scarcely for a righteous man will one die: yet peradventure for a good man some would even dare to die. But God commendeth his love toward us, in that, while we were yet sinners, Christ died for us (Romans 5:6–8).

THE PREVIOUS TWO CHAPTERS discussed the grounds, the soil, or the condition of our heart when the seed of knowledge, the promise, the revelation of God's word is sown. However, if we are to receive the seed upon good soil, we must comprehend God's love.

Without understanding the love of God, we cannot possibly receive the seed of knowledge on good soil. Our heart is not prepared to withstand storms, obstacles, strategies of Satan, or dark times without believing that God's love is there to help us through this hardship, grief, adversity, or trial that has shrouded us in darkness.

> For I am persuaded, that neither death, nor life, nor angels, nor principalities, nor powers, nor things present, nor things to come, Nor height, nor depth, nor any other creature, shall be able to separate us from the love of God, which is in Christ Jesus our Lord (Romans 8:38–39).

GOD'S LOVE IS KEY TO GOOD SOIL

It is imperative that we believe God's love for us is so great that nothing can separate us from him. He promises to be with us always, even unto the end of the world (Matthew 28:20). We are never in any dark time alone. It is not what we feel, but what we know. Whether we sense his presence or not, faith knows He is always with us.

> Thy word is a lamp unto my feet, and a light unto my path (Psalm 119:105).

When we comprehend God's love, we realize that his word is our light to guide us through the darkness of trials. We know we cannot walk outside at night without a light. There could be many things to trip us, unseen holes to cause us to stumble, unknown predators, etc. Well, as God's soldiers, we are constantly walking through a shroud of evil bent on destroying us.

Without a knowledge of God's love and his word, we have no light or way to overcome the darkness trying to crush us. We walk through a dark and evil world and God's word will help us evade the traps that have been set by the enemy to ambush us. Although we may see no light, with an understanding of his ever-presence and endless love, we believe his word. Without the light of his word to lighten our path through the dark time, we will stumble.

What do I mean that his word is our light to get us through? He promises that we can do all things through Christ which strengthens us (Philippians 4:13). It does not matter how dark the storm, how weak we may feel, or how strong our adversary appears. God promises to give us the strength to get through or confront whatever we may face in this life. That verse in Philippians is our light. We know He loves us, for that was proven on Calvary (John 3:16). We know He is always with us (Hebrews 13:5; Matthew 28:20). Thus, we quote his promise, his seed, his *light* until we are out of the darkness.

I am not saying it will be immediate, a week, a month, etc. It will end in the fullness of his time. If there were not the danger of us giving up, there would be no strengthening of our faith. Every storm has the potential to overthrow us. How can we overcome if there is nothing to overcome?

Seeds of Knowledge

In my book, *Storms Are Faith's Workout: Preparing Christians For Spiritual Ambush*, I gave an enlightening study of God's love in Chapter 3. I will not redo that chapter, but I will use some of its points concerning the Tabernacle in the wilderness to enrich its understanding to emphasize the necessity for good soil.

> And thou shalt love the Lord thy God with all thy heart, and with all thy soul, and with all thy mind, and with all thy strength: this is the first commandment (Mark 12:30).
>
> And he said to them all, If any man will come after me, let him deny himself, and take up his cross daily and follow me. For whosoever will save his life shall lose it: but whosoever will lose his life for my sake, the same shall save it (Luke 9:23-24).

We can never love God with our whole being unless we choose to deny self. To deny self means to wrestle with what we want verses what God wants. If this life is more important than the next one, we will do whatever we can to protect it. Everything we do, say, and think will center on this life. We will never choose to do anything which might endanger our safety, our health, or our comfort. However, if following Christ is more important, we will find ourselves in unsafe, unhealthy, and uncomfortable situations. We may risk death, but we will not fear it. God's soldiers do not fear death, because we know to be absent from the body is to be present with the Lord (2 Corinthians 5:8). We renounce this life because we covet life with him.

We have the love for God, the love for people, the love for money, the love for things, the love for fame, etc. Unless we understand our HEART has many threads or strings pulling on it, we will not comprehend the importance of loving God and believing He loves us. The key to God's seed falling upon good soil is contingent upon that knowledge.

Since our life is composed of threads attached to our heart that can break us when under duress or extreme difficulties, what occurs is dependent upon the condition of our heart at the time when darkness falls upon us, and which thread is the strongest. Will God's seed fall by the wayside, on stony ground, among thorns, or on good soil? There is only one thread that will keep us through the loss of all the others, and that is the love for God.

Let me help us understand the importance of our love for God being the strongest thread. When I lost someone without any warning, I felt the carpet was pulled out from under my feet. My whole life became devastated. It was like I had no foundation to stand upon. My mind was flooded with questions upon questions. My heart was overwhelmed. My emotions were shattered. It was a storm out to annihilate my faith. I closed myself in a room trying to find light in the darkness. I cried out to the Lord for grace, for I was undone. He said I had the grace sufficient to get me through, for his strength is made perfect in my weakness (2 Corinthians 12:9).

It was the light of God's word that He would never leave nor forsake me that started me to sense my foundation. The truth that I could live without the person, but I cannot live without the Lord, brought peace to my turmoil. No, I did not stop grieving my loss, but the love for God was the thread to my heart that kept me afloat and helped me heal in time.

Through that, I learned that if the love for God is stronger than any other loves, it will be the strong thread that will support us through the loss of all else. That is why He wants us to love him with all our heart, with all our soul, with all our mind, and with all our strength (Mark 12:30). It is not because God is egotistic, but because He knows our life will be faced with many dark storms. If the strongest thread to our heart is love for him, we will get through any dark, fierce, furious, and violent storm.

The devil is always looking for an opportunity to convince us God doesn't love us. He is ever lurking and waiting for that weak moment when we might doubt God's love. He will instigate us to question if God loves us, why is He allowing such darkness to consume us, why did He take him/her when we prayed for healing, why are we in such a financial dilemma, why is our son/daughter serving the devil, why was there no warning before the storm?

Whatever darts of doubt Satan can wield our way is his full time vendetta. He hates God and hates all who worship him. In truth, Satan hates all mankind because of the love God has for us.

Seeds of Knowledge

Jesus didn't die on the cross of Calvary for the angels and demons. He died on that cross for us who were alienated from God.

His love for us was so great that while we were enemies of God, Christ died on the cross. His death was the only way we could be reconciled to God. In other words, while we were set in our sinful life, Christ loved us so much that He died so we could be set free from our sins and be reconciled to God.

If the devil can get us to doubt God's love, we will not love him. If we do not love God, it will not be our strongest thread. We will never enter in at the straight gate and narrow way which leads to life that only a few find. Instead, we will continue on the wide and broad path that leads to Hell that the multitude is entering in at (Matthew 7:13–14).

The soil in which the seed is sown is determined upon the degree of our love for God and our comprehension of his love for us. That is why so many hearts are not good soil. Our heart is the wayside where Satan steals the seed sown. Our heart is the stony ground where the persecution, affliction for the word comes, we are offended. Our heart is the thorns where the cares of this world, the deceitfulness of riches, or the lust of the flesh, the lust of the eyes, and the pride of life cause us to become unfruitful. Only the love of God will cause us to have good soil that brings forth fruit.

In *Storms Are Faith's Workout*, I used the Tabernacle in the Wilderness in chapter three to describe why some never fully comprehend God's love and never love him with their whole being. I explained that I never grasped the truth of God's love for me until I entered the inner covering. It illuminated why the Apostle John could claim to be the disciple whom Jesus loved. That revelation supercharged my understanding of God's love. I suggest reading the book to get under the inner covering and receive the knowledge of God's love.

For this book, I want to use those examples to reveal the four types of soil upon which the Lord sows his seed and its results. Instead of going from the inner to outer like I did in *Storms Are Faith's Workout*, I will begin with the outer to the inner. That will enable us to see the different soils upon which the seed of knowledge, promise, or revelation is sown according Mark 4: 3–20.

WAYSIDE IS THE OUTER COVERING OF BADGER SKINS

The outer or third covering was made of badger skin. This covering portrayed Jesus as the suffering and rejected savior of Isaiah 53. He is seen as one who had no beauty that He would be desired. If we see no beauty in God's seed of knowledge, we will not give it much thought. Therefore, the seed will have no impact upon our thinking, and we will reject its entrance into our heart.

Anyway, the badger skin represents a rejection or a resistance. If our heart rejects or resists God's word, his promise, or his revelation at the time it is sown, it will fall by the wayside and immediately be snatched up by Satan.

Biblical Example

35) And Jesus said unto them, I am the bread of life: he that cometh to me shall never hunger; and he that believeth on me shall never thirst. 47) Verily, verily, I say unto you, He that believeth on me hath everlasting life. 48) I am the bread of life. 51) I am the living bread which came down from heaven: if any man eat of this bread, he shall live for ever: and the bread that I will give is my flesh, which I will give for the life of the world. 53) Then Jesus said unto them, Verily, verily, I say unto you, Except ye eat the flesh of the Son of man, and drink his blood, ye have no life in you. 54) Whoso eateth my flesh, and drinketh my blood, hath eternal life; and I will raise him up at the last day. 55) For my flesh is meat indeed, and my blood is drink indeed. 56) He that eateth my flesh, and drinketh my blood, dwelleth in me, and I in him. 57) As the living Father hath sent me, and I live by the Father: so he that eateth me, even he shall live by me. 58) This is that bread which came down from heaven: not as your fathers did eat manna, and are dead: he that eateth of this bread shall live for ever. 60) Many therefore of his disciples, when they had heard this, said, This is an hard saying; who can bear it. 63) It is the spirit that

> quickeneth; the flesh profiteth nothing: the words that I speak unto you, they are spirit, and they are life. 66) From that time many of his disciples went back, and walked no more with him (John 6:35, 47–66).

In this discourse of Christ, He gives a hard saying that did not rest with some of his disciples, who were troubled at such a statement. Their flesh cringed at drinking blood, for to the Jews drinking blood was a major offense.

However, they took his meaning literally when it was meant spiritually. In verse 51, Jesus stated, "I am the living bread which came down from heaven: if any man eat of this bread, he shall live for ever."

Earlier in verse 35, Jesus said, "I am the bread of life: he that cometh to me shall never hunger; and he that believeth on me shall never thirst." Now, in verse 63, Jesus says, "The words that I speak unto you, they are spirit, and they are life."

Jesus is the written word made flesh. In other words, Jesus is the living word and the Bible is the written word. What Jesus was saying had to be spiritually discerned. Those who were not prepared in their hearts to receive hard sayings rejected or resisted such words.

This example is to show God's soldiers the importance, the necessity, the requirement of studying God's word. Without an understanding of the whole of scripture, our heart will reject or resist whatever is uncomfortable, difficult, distressing, and unpleasant on our flesh.

Jesus was teaching that we are to be united in him by believing in his death (the sacrifice of his flesh) and his resurrection, and by devoting ourselves as living sacrifices to God. We do this by living according to his word and depending upon the Holy Spirit for guidance and power.

We continue to experience the benefits of salvation by *remaining* in a devoted relationship with Christ and by the continuous feeding on God's word. It is spiritually dangerous for us to pull away from following Christ because we cannot accept a hard saying in his word.

How many of God's soldiers have allowed Satan to steal seeds of knowledge, promises, and revelations because we reject or resist a hard saying in the word?

STONY GROUND IS SECOND COVERING OF RAM'S SKIN

The covering under the badger's skin was made of ram's skin and dyed red. This speaks of the blood Jesus shed for us, and it represents his sacrifice for sin. We know Jesus shed his blood for us, but we do not recognize his fullness, because we stop here. Staying here means we are still living in guilt of our past sins. We have never gone past the fact that when we accepted Christ, our sins were blotted out by his blood. We do not comprehend the fact that He was our sin bearer and escape goat. We do not realize our sins are completely taken away. We do not understand what is forgiven is forgotten. The enemy comes along and throws our past sins at us and we are kept out of the fullness of God's love and continue to live in guilt.

Okay, how does that reveal the stony ground? We accept the seed of knowledge gladly, but never realize his love has wiped our sins clean. Thus, we never have roots into God's love. Instead, we continuously are kept under by affliction and persecution about our past sins. Because we are under constant persecution concerning our past, we never comprehend God's love and never enjoy our freedom in Christ.

This covering represents any persecution or affliction because of Christ or his word. Because we have no root in ourselves, we endure for a time. We may even seem like we are strong believers, but when faced with persecution, affliction, etc. for Christ or his word, we are offended. In other words, we have no roots to withstand the heat of persecution and are easily plucked up.

Biblical Example

They say unto the blind man again, What sayest thou of him, that he hath opened thine eyes? He said, He is a prophet. But the Jews did not believe concerning him, that he had been blind, and received his sight, until they called the parents of him that had received his sight. And they asked them, saying, Is this your son, who ye say was born blind? How then doth he now see? His parents answered them and said, We know that this is our son, and that he was born blind: But by what means he now seeth, we know not: or who hath opened his eyes, we know not: he is of age; ask him: he shall speak for himself. These words spake his parents, because they feared the Jews: for the Jews had agreed already, that if any man did confess that he was Christ, he should be put out of the synagogue. Therefore said his parents, he is of age; ask him (John 9:17–23).

In these verses, we find the parents of the blind man who had been healed by Jesus being interrogated by the Pharisees. The Jews did not believe the blind man had been blind, so they brought in his parents.

Here we find them willing to claim their son was born blind, but would say no more. Instead they told the Jews to ask their son who was of age to answer for himself.

Why would they not admit about his healing? Verse 22 informs us they feared the Jews, for the Jews had agreed that any who confessed Jesus was Christ would be put out of the synagogue.

What's the big deal of being put out or excommunicated from the synagogue? To the Jew, the synagogue was the center of Jewish community life. The persecution for such a move would mean being unable to work, probably kicked out of their home, forced to live as outsiders, being cast out of social relationships. Because they had no roots in God's love, they were not willing to stand against the persecution for Christ.

How many of God's soldiers are denying Christ daily because we do not stand up for him or his word to avoid persecution or affliction?

THORNS IS THE FIRST COVERING OF GOAT'S HAIR

This covering covered the inner covering and it was made of goat's hair. It was larger than the inner veil so that it completely covered the inner covering. This suggests at this covering, the fullness of Christ's heavenly character is not seen. We have grasped hold of the truth that Christ is our escape goat or sin bearer and walk free of the guilt of forgiven sin. Yet, we have not entered into the fullness or the full relationship God desires us to have in Christ. We comprehend Christ took away our sins and He is our escape goat. We know we are now forgiven and are no longer guilty of our forgiven sins, but we do not know the beauty of God's love for us. Love for God is not our strongest thread.

This ground reveals that we are not free from other entanglements or the other threads attached to our hearts. We are missing so much in our Christian journey. We can be besieged by the cares of this world, the deceitfulness of riches, and the lusts of other things. Our heart is not detached from whatever can take precedence over Christ. The other threads or strings are stronger than our love for God. At any time, we can be overwhelmed by the other threads and bear no fruit.

Biblical Example:

Cares of this world (life)

> And Jacob sod pottage: and Esau came from the field, and he was faint: And Esau said to Jacob, Feed me, I pray thee, with that same red pottage; for I am faint: therefore was his name called Edom, And Jacob said, Sell me this day thy birthright. And Esau said, Behold, I am at the point to die: and what profit shall this birthright do to me? And Jacob said, Swear to me this day; and he sware unto him: and he sold his birthright unto Jacob (Genesis 25:29–33).
>
> Lest there be any fornicator, or profane person, as Esau, who for one morsel of meat sold his birthright (Hebrews 12:16).

Esau was more concerned about his life than the value of his birthright. Instead of believing God would have given him the strength to get home, he was willing to sell his birthright.

Are we comprehending what Esau did? Do we realize that he had the birthright that would have made it Abraham, Isaac, and Esau? Yet, he thought more of his fleshly desire for food than his spiritual inheritance.

Esau was profane because he willingly cast off the birthright for indulgence in temporary pleasure. He gave up his birthright for fleshly gratification. He cared for his life more than his relationship with God. So, to satisfy his hunger, he sold his birthright for "a single meal."

How many of God's soldiers are selling our birthright for a temporary indulgence of our flesh because we care more about this life than the next?

Deceitfulness of riches

> And a certain ruler asked him, saying, Good Master, what shall I do to inherit eternal life? And Jesus said unto him, Why callest thou me good? none is good, save one, that is, God: Thou knowest the commandments, Do not commit adultery, Do not kill, Do not steal, Do not bear false witness, Honour thy father and thy mother. And he said, All these have I kept from my youth up. Now when Jesus heard these things, he said unto him, Yet lackest thou one thing: sell all that thou hast, and distribute unto the poor, and thou shalt have treasure in heaven: and come, follow me. And when he heard this, he was very sorrowful: for he was very rich (Luke 18:18–23).

This young rich ruler was more interested in wealth on earth than building up treasure in heaven. He was under the belief that riches were his security. Jesus went to the heart of the matter to expose that his wealth was the only possession keeping him from following Christ.

Jesus says in Matthew 6:21, "For where your treasure is, there will your heart be also." This man's heart belonged to his riches and not to God.

He was not willing to put Christ above his possessions. If we are to follow Christ, we must be willing to deny what we want and choose God's will. It means placing kingdom matters and discipleship above personal possessions. To the young man, the cost of discipleship was too high. He was not willing to give up his riches.

This parable is not teaching that God's people are to be poor. It is revealing that we must be willing to give up anything that Christ asks us to. What we possess must never get in the way of our relationship with God. This young man was more concerned about following his wealth than following Christ.

How many of God's soldiers are coveting more money at the neglect of our relationship with Christ?

The lusts of other things entering in

> Nevertheless among the chief rulers also many believed on him; but because of the Pharisees they did not confess him, lest they should be put out of the synagogue: For they loved the praise of men more than the praise of God (John 12:42–43).

This could also be used to show they feared being put out of the synagogue and the persecution, ridicule, affliction of confessing Jesus. However, I believe this reveals what happens to many of God's soldiers today.

In these verses, we see the main reason for their not confessing Christ was they loved the praise of men more than the praise of God. The lust of other things entering in was the honor and approval of people (family, spouse, children, employer, associates, friends, etc.), and it kept them quiet about their belief in Christ. In fact, they denied Christ before men, and Christ would deny them before his Father in heaven (Matthew 10:33).

How many of God's soldiers allow the desire or lust of man's approval cause us to not denounce sin, cause us to compromise, and cause us to be closet Christians?

GOOD GROUND IS THE INNER COVERING

The inner covering was beautiful and costly. It was a splendid piece of tapestry embroidered with blue, scarlet, and gold with cherubs on it. But the only way to see that inner veil or inner covering was to be inside the tabernacle. We cannot experience the beauty of Christ's love unless we are completely immersed in him. The inner covering is a type of the fullness, the beauty, the heavenly character of Jesus that cannot be seen or understood until completely engulfed in his love.

This covering was completely covered and hidden from the view of the people. God so covered its beauty under skins and curtains that its glories and beauty of spiritual things are only seen when we enter into the fullness of God's love. Only as we immerse ourselves in Christ can we experience such wondrous love. His love causes us to be awe stricken that God Almighty could love us so much that He would die for us and take our punishment for sin.

His selfless and self-sacrificing love causes our hearts to cry, "Abba, Father, not my will but thine be done." We have a deep inner desire to always do those things that please him.

In here, we have learned to deny self what it wants. We have learned to love God with all our heart, with all our soul, with all our mind, and with all our strength. Because we comprehend that no storm, obstacle, or Satanic strategy can separate us from God's love, we have strengthened the thread of our love for God so that it is stronger than any other thread to our heart. Nothing/no one comes between us and our God.

Under the inner covering, we are enabled to experience the beauty of God's love. We walk daily in his love and bring forth fruit some thirty-fold, some sixty, and some an hundred.

Biblical Example

Of the Jews five times received I forty stripes save one. Thrice was I beaten with rods, once was I stoned, thrice I suffered shipwreck, a night and a day I have been in the deep; In journeyings, often, in perils of waters, in perils of robbers, in perils by mine own countrymen, in perils by the heathen, in perils in the city, in perils in the wilderness, in perils in the sea, in perils among false brethren; In weariness and painfulness, in watchings, often, in hunger and thirst, in fastings often, in cold and nakedness. Beside those things that are without, that which cometh upon me daily, the care of all the churches (2 Corinthians 11: 24–28).

But what things were gain to me, those I counted loss for Christ. Yea doubtless, and I count all things but loss for the excellency of the knowledge of Christ Jesus my Lord: for whom I have suffered the loss of all things, and do count them but dung, that I may win Christ (Philippians 3:8).

The Apostle Paul was so devoted to the Lord that he willingly suffered the loss of all things for the knowledge of Christ. Whatever it cost him to know Christ better, he considered them as rubbish. His heart craved to know Christ and to experience his personal presence and companionship in a more intimate way.

Paul had suffered much in his service to Christ. His life was one of constant tribulation; he suffered much difficulty, affliction, distress, and trouble as a result of his work for Christ. Yet, he knew that through it all, the love of God was always with him. Although no man stood with him and all forsook him, the Lord stood with him and strengthened him (2 Timothy 4:16–17).

Let me explain this. The persecution was severe against Christians, and few found the courage to identify with someone as faithful and outspoken as Paul. Their love was not centered upon Christ, but on their own life. Fear overruled faith.

It takes a courage so rooted in God's love that will stand against the evil of the day. When seed is sown on this good ground, the personal price paid for Christ and others brings forth fruit some thirty-fold, some sixty, and some an hundred.

How many of God's soldiers are so rooted in God's love, that we are willing to suffer the loss of all things, count them as nothing, to experience Christ presence and companionship?

Once we comprehend God's love and Christ's sacrifice for us, we are overwhelmed by that love. Which one of us would die for an enemy? Which one of us would sacrifice self for those who hate us? Yet, that is what Christ did for us.

The revelation of God's love so humbles us that we are willing to do whatever pleases him. We no longer place more value on our physical life, but are more concerned with spiritual or eternal life. Our focus centers upon our need for him and that without him we have nothing of value in this life.

> That he would grant you, according to the riches of his glory, to be strengthened with might by his Spirit in the inner man; That Christ may dwell in your hearts by faith; that ye, being rooted and grounded in love, May be able to comprehend with all the saints what is the breadth, and length, and depth, and height; And to know the love of Christ, which passeth knowledge, that ye might be filled with all the fulness of God (Ephesians 3:16–19).

The love of Christ surpasses all our knowledge. Paul reveals that it reaches every aspect of our life. It is boundless, endless, exhaustless, and measureless. God's love continues the *length* of our lives. It is *deep* enough to reach the depths of discouragement, despair, grief, and even death. It covers the *breadth* of our personal experiences and reaches out to the whole world. It rises to the *heights* of our jubilation (Ephesians 3:19).

It is through the love of Christ that we can know the love of God. It was God's love that gave Christ for our redemption. It was Christ's love for us that induced him to give his life's blood for our salvation.

Romans 5:8 says that Christ died for us while we were yet sinners. Those words are amazing and overwhelming. God sent Christ to die for us, not because we were good enough. Christ died because

He loved us so much and did not want to leave us in that alienated, estranged, separated state.

Do we comprehend the gift of Christ to us is the measure of God's love, and the death of Christ for us is the measure of Christ's love? Simply put, Jesus is the love of God wrapped in skin. As we grasp hold of that truth, we are enlightened to the immense love God has for us.

His love caused him to willingly be nailed to that cross, be separated from his loving Father, and die that cruel death for us. When the devil tries to influence us to question or feel uncertain about God's love, we must remember that He loved us even before we turned to him.

Comprehending such love causes us to be humbled. We are overwhelmed that God could love us that much and a love for him rises up in us like a steaming volcano. With that kind of love for God, all other threads have no power over our heart to destroy our love for Christ.

Being rooted and grounded in the love of God, our soil is good ground. All seeds of knowledge, promises, or revelations of God are now enabled to bring forth fruit some thirty-fold, some sixty, and some an hundred!

Chapter 4

God Cannot Be Compared

To whom will ye liken God? or what likeness will ye compare unto him? The workman melteth a graven image, and goldsmith spreadeth it over with gold, and casteth silver chains. He that is so impoverished that he hath no oblation chooseth a tree that will not rot; he seeketh unto him a cunning workman to prepare a graven image, that shall not be moved. Have ye not known? have ye not heard? hath it not been told you from the beginning? have ye not understood from the foundations of the earth? It is he that sitteth upon the circle of the earth, and inhabitants thereof are as grasshoppers; that stretcheth out the heavens as a curtain, and spreadeth them out as a tent to dwell in: That bringeth the princes to nothing; he maketh the judges of the earth as vanity. Yea, they shall not be planted; yea, they shall not be sown: yea, their stock shall not take root in the earth: and he shall also blow upon them, and they shall wither, and the whirlwind shall take them away as stubble. To whom then will ye liken me; or shall I be equal? saith the Holy One. Lift up your eyes on high, and behold who hath created these things, that bringeth out their host by number: he calleth them all by names by the greatness of his might, for that he is strong in power; not one faileth (Isaiah 40:18–26).

GOD CANNOT BE COMPARED

WITH AN UNDERSTANDING OF God's love, beginning with this chapter, we will endeavor to expound how the seeds of knowledge or God's word will enable us to sow on good ground. Since our heart is the soil in which God sows his seed, the more we know and understand about God and his love, the more our ground will be prepared to receive the seed for harvest.

All the comparisons Isaiah had been introducing up to verse eighteen lead to the unavoidable and inevitable conclusion that God is the true God and that beside him there is no other. I mean who else can measure the waters in the hollow of his hand, and mete out heaven with the span, comprehend the dust of the earth in a measure, weigh the mountains in scales, and the hills in a balance? Who else directs the Spirit of the Lord, or being his counselor has taught him? With whom did He counsel with? Who instructed him and taught him the path of judgment? Who taught him knowledge and showed him the way of understanding? (Isaiah 40:12-14)

> *To whom then will ye liken God? or what likeness will ye compare unto him (40:18)?*

In order to establish the truth of God, Isaiah asks a question. A question is always more forceful than stating the truth in a simple declaratory or explanatory sentence. If we stated it instead of asking, we would say: God cannot be compared with anyone or anything.

To whom will you liken God or what likeness will you compare him with? Asking that question forces us to be faced with truth, thereby answerable to such. Truth confronted and answered in truth must declare that there can be no comparison between the living eternal God and any man, for man is but a creation.

Man is limited, finite, temporal; God is infinite, eternal, and unchangeable in all his attributes and perfections. God's soldiers must comprehend for truth to be truth in us, we must always remember the infinite or endless distance between God and us. We must keep this truth in our heart and mind, lest we make the gulf less than what it is. If we forget, we could be tempted to bring God down to the level of his creation.

Many today believe man is a god or can obtain godhood. To break down the distinction or the truth of the infinite distance between God and man is to fall into the sin of idolatry. We change the truth of God into a lie, and worship and serve the creature or creation more than the Creator (Romans 1:25). How many put God as the servant? How many tell him what He should do, how He should do it, and when He should do it? Whenever we forget the Sovereignty of God, we bring him down below his creation.

He becomes servant and we become master. Of course that is only in our mind, for God is the one who sits upon a throne, high and lifted up, and his train fills the temple (Isaiah 6:1). It is God who is high and lifted up above all his creation. Good soil keeps that truth in its heart and keeps God as Creator and remembers we are his creation.

> *The workman melteth a graven image, and the goldsmith spreadeth it over with gold, and casteth silver chains (40:19).*

In this verse, Isaiah begins his condemnation against the idols. Comparing God with idols is sacrilege or irreverence. The prophets main objective is to cause us to comprehend that God cannot be compared. How do we compare infinite with finite, unlimited with limited, Creator with creation? We cannot compare God with man. We cannot visit heaven. Yet, God is everywhere at all times (Psalms 139:8). We cannot speak worlds into existence. Yet, God spoke all things into existence (Hebrews 11:3). There is nothing that we see in this physical universe that existed before God declared them. The words went out of his mouth and they suddenly came to pass (Isaiah 48:3).

If we compare God to his creation, we are trying to bring the Almighty down to our level. The teachings of the cults, occults, New Age, Mormonism, etc. are nothing new. Isaiah's active ministry took place about 745–695 B. C., which is about 2,700 years ago. Way back then, God was teaching against idol or self worship.

The main thrust or vital point being brought out through Isaiah is a warning to man, God wants us to know that He is above and beyond all his creation. It is essential for us to know and understand the *infinite distance* between God and his creation. It's sort of like the vast difference between the employer and the employee. One is above and the other is subservient.

GOD CANNOT BE COMPARED

God is master and we are servant. With that mentality, our thinking is kept in the proper perspective. He is always above us. We cannot ever reach his status or come close to it. How can that which is created ever be greater than its Creator? It cannot, and we cannot. How can that which is created tell its Creator what to do. It cannot, and we cannot.

Isaiah declares that God cannot be compared with anyone, and He cannot be compared with idols. How foolish is man to bring down the eternal God into the temporal realm in the form of an idol. Think about that. Even the material used in the manufacturing of an idol was created by God himself.

Who created the hands the man uses to gather the material from the earth? Who created the hands forming or making the idol? How ludicrous to believe the Creator of those hands can be molded into a god.

> *He that is so impoverished that he hath no oblation chooseth a tree that will not rot; he seeketh unto him a cunning workman to prepare a graven image, that shall not be moved (40:20).*

In this verse, we find the impoverished or poor man so obsessed with having his own idol, that he will one way or the other find money to procure the choicest materials, and the help of the best artist to make his idol.

Think about that. No matter how poor, he will take money to purchase the best idol that has no benefit to his life. Look at the alcoholic, drug addict, the gambler, etc. Their idol is so important to them that they spend whatever money they have to worship it. Yet, it has no ability to better their life. If fact, their idol is self-destructive.

The sad part is it costs more than money when we worship an idol; it costs our soul. It can also cost the loss of a job, a spouse, children, family, home, reputation, etc. Furthermore, our lack of serving God and worshipping our idol can cost the souls of those we should be bringing to the Lord.

> *Have ye not known? have ye not heard? hath it not been told you from the beginning? have ye not understood from the foundations of the earth (40:21)?*

In this verse, we are asked, *have ye not heard or will ye not hear?* Isaiah tells us the truth that God is proclaimed to us by the living voice of the prophets. Why do we continue in darkness and deafness? Why are we unwilling to hear the actual state of the case?

I believe the prophet is bewildered at man's folly. He knows our ignorance is not due to a lack of hearing the truth, for it has been told time and time again. The truth that God is Creator is not hidden nor has it not been declared to his children. Throughout the history of the entire race of men, God's revelation was in the world and was proclaimed to man.

Then Isaiah takes it further than the mouth of the prophets declaring God's truth. Even without that revelation of God being declared, his whole creation, the earth itself should cause men to understand that God is the Creator.

> For the invisible things of him from the creation of the world are clearly seen, being understood by the things that are made, even his eternal power and Godhead; so that they are without excuse (Romans 1:20).

Nature reveals God's character and personal qualities. Although the Fall distorted the creation with thorns and thistles, God's order and beauty are still visible. Through nature, we see a God of intellect, power, and who controls powerful forces.

> *It is he that sitteth upon the circle of the earth, and the inhabitants thereof are as grasshoppers; that stretcheth out the heavens as a curtain, and spreadeth them out as a tent to dwell in (40:22).*

Isaiah is stating that what they have heard and what they have seen in the creation should have taught them that it is God who sits upon the circle of the earth.

The phrase "sitteth upon the circle of the earth" is a figurative expression revealing God's providential upholding and maintaining of creation. We would not be too impressed with the knowledge that God is Creator unless God continually upheld his creation.

> Who being the brightness of his glory, and the express image of his person, and upholding all things by the

word of his power, when he had by himself purged our sins, sat down on the right hand of the Majesty on high (Hebrews 1:3).

This is amazing. The power that spoke the universe into existence is the same power that keeps it operating with precise movement. As his word spoke and it was, He speaks, and all things are kept intact by his word. In other words, the earth turns on its axis according to his word. The planets all rotate according to his word. The sun, moon, stars, etc. all stay in place according to his word.

As God is seated upon his high throne, men appear as grasshoppers. In their actions and activities men are as weak and powerless as the grasshoppers. In all their multitude, they cannot hold the world in its course.

If grasshoppers (men) cannot do it, how much less anything that is made by grasshoppers (men)? This comparison shows the folly of idolatry.

God compares man's actions and activities, the power of man concerning this universe, with the weakness and powerlessness of a grasshopper in upholding this world. Yet how many teach that man is like God because he was created in God's image?

> I am the Lord, and there is none else, there is no God beside me: I girded thee, though thou hast not known me: That they may know from the rising of the sun, and from the west, that there is none beside me, I am the Lord, and there is none else (Isaiah 45:5-6).

Created in God's image or not will never make man God. God makes clear that He is the only God. All the created universe and all in it is in his hand and his control. Man cannot control how the universe operates. Man is not the creator of the universe. Man is part of the creation by the Creator.

> *That bringeth the princes to nothing; he maketh the judges of the earth as vanity (40:23).*

Even the princes and judges or the rulers of this earth do not have their position in their own power. The one who is really active in permitting rulers to occupy seats of authority is God himself.

Princes, judges, and all others who oppose the divine plan, regardless of their wealth and power, are no real hindrance to God. He is able to remove and make them as nothing to accomplish his will.

> Yea, they shall not be planted; yea, they shall not be sown: yea, their stock shall not take root in the earth: and he shall also blow upon them, and they shall wither, and the whirlwind shall take them away as stubble (40:24).

The whirlwind will take them away as stubble. Depending upon God's purpose, rulers are here one moment and gone the next. Whatever power they have was given to them by God, and even then, it is but for a season.

God rules from eternity to eternity and no one has given him his power, and no one can put him out of his throne. As He created, He can destroy. For with God nothing is impossible (Luke 1:37).

> To whom then will ye like me, or shall I be equal?saith the Holy One. Lift up your eyes on high, and behold who hath created these things, that bringeth out their host by number: he calleth them all by names by the greatness of his might, for that he is strong in power; not one faileth (40:25-26).

Isaiah ends his argument against idolatry in any form by reverting back to verse 18. It is identical to that verse, except here, God himself is the speaker.

He points us toward the heavens as proof of his existence and perfection. The heavens demonstrate his greatness and power. Only a master mind can keep all things moving with precision, so that not one fails.

We must comprehend that we cannot compare God to anything or anyone. He is creator, is superior to all his creation, and all idols made by the hands of his creation are powerless. Our comprehension of the majesty of God causes our heart to be good soil, receive the sown word, and bring forth fruit some thirty-fold, some sixty, and some an hundred!

Chapter 5

Belief In God's Word Determines Soil

And this is the confidence that we have in him, that, if we ask any thing according to his will, he heareth us: And if we know that he hear us, whatsoever we ask, we know that we have the petitions that we desired of him (1 John 5:14–15).

THIS CHAPTER IS MEANT to illuminate why prayers are not always answered according to what we ask. A lack of understanding concerning this truth is why our soil can become other than good ground. We quote, "And whatsoever ye ask in my name, that will I do, that the Father may be glorified in the Son" (John 14:13). Then when it is not answered, we can allow our heart to become discouraged.

A lack of knowledge of the whole of Scripture is the reason for our heart to become other than good ground. The scripture reference in 1 John states IF we ask anything according to his will, He will hear us. It does not state if we ask anything according to our will, He hears us. When we pray, we are not to request what we want. We are to petition for his will. Whenever we align our prayers according to his will, He will hear. If He hears, we can be certain we will receive our petition. That is confidence or assurance. In other words, we can bank on it.

How do we pray according to God's will? How do we even know what his will is? It is quite simple. His will is anything that He has promised in his word. The word of God is the revelation of the will of God. Whatever God has promised, we are justified in expecting. What He has promised, and we expect is what we are to pray for.

> But without faith it is impossible to please him: for he that cometh to God must believe that he is, and that he is a rewarder of them that diligently seek him (Hebrews 11:6).

We are now satisfied that He hears our prayer of faith, requesting the things which God himself has promised, and we expect the prayer petitioned to be answered.

> Now faith is the substance of things hoped for, the evidence of things not seen (Hebrews 11:1).

Our faith is our substance, our support, our subsistence. Faith is our foundation for another thing to stand on. The evidence of what we hope for is not based on what we visibly see. Since we believe God is, we have prayed according to his word, we know He heard us, our faith sees what is not visible in the natural. We know our prayer is answered in the supernatural. Now, we wait for the harvest.

> God is not a man, that he should lie; neither the son of man, that he should repent: hath he said, and shall he not do it? or hath he spoken, and shall he not make it good? (Numbers 23:19).

Let's continue to reveal the assurance that is in God's word. The above scripture informs us that God is a person of his word. That's the only way to put it. Before we were saved and after salvation, we have never had respect for anyone who would say something and didn't keep his/her word.

We expect if someone's word is to be worth anything, it must be kept. I have always believed that we are only as good as our word. If our word is not kept, how can we be respected?

BELIEF IN GOD'S WORD DETERMINES SOIL

When we proclaim one thing and we do not do it, we are a hypocrite. We are a liar. However, we never have to be concerned about that with God. He is a person of his word. If He promises us something in his word, He will do it. We do not have to doubt. We do not have to wonder about it. We have the proof in the scriptures. Our Bible is a diary of the different ones who diligently followed God. In each case, what God promised them, He performed.

Whatever He has promised to us who receive his promise on good ground, He will do it. He is God and He cannot lie. He will fulfill each and every promise that we receive by faith and bring forth its fruit.

God is omnipotent or all powerful. Do we comprehend that his being all powerful means there is not a power that is greater than the power of God? He is the all-powerful one. He is the one that surpasses any kind of power. Every other power was created by him, who is the super power. He is truly the only super hero, for there is none other.

Why are many claiming to be Christians not bringing forth fruit? Why is God's word or seed of knowledge not being sown on good soil? How many are believing the devil's lies? Why are those who are supposed to be God's soldiers not revealing the power of God? It's quite simple. Many are sitting on doubt and unbelief, and not believing what God has promised He is able to perform.

Too many of God's people are not studying his word. It is left on a shelf, table, etc. Instead of searching the scriptures to know what we believe and why we believe it, we listen to others. We take their word for it without Holy Ghost revelation.

Because we do not know the word, we do not know how to pray. We pray according to our whims, wants, desires, lusts and wonder why we do not receive. God makes clear that He will always hear and answer whatever we ask according to his will.

We must know the scriptures and be led by the Holy Spirit in praying. The Holy Spirit knows the mind and will of God, and when we yield to him, He will lead us to pray according to the will of God.

It is God who calleth those things which be not as though they were (Romans 4:17). That is who God is. Hebrews 11:1 says "Now" which means right at this moment, this very instance, as I stand here, right now.

God is telling us whatever He has promised us, it is NOW completed by faith. If we lose faith, we lose the promise. We must understand that. As I have taught in my other books, the time from seedtime (sowing) until harvest (reaping) has no set period. Our faith will be sorely tested from seed to fruit.

If our heart is not assured of God's word, the seed of knowledge, promise, etc. will be sown by the wayside, on stony ground, or among thorns.

> Knowing this first, that there shall come in the last days scoffers, walking after their own lusts, And saying, Where is the promise of his coming? for since the fathers fell asleep, all things continue as they were from the beginning of the creation. For this they willingly are ignorant of, that by the word of God the heavens were of old, and the earth standing out of the water and in the water: Whereby the world that then was, being overflowed with water, perished (2 Peter 3:3–6).

The devil comes at us like the scoffers during seedtime and harvest. We are to know this first. We are to know that in the last days, or the time we are in at present, that scoffers walking after their own lusts will question or mock God's word. These are willingly ignorant that the word of God created the heavens of old.

The heavens came into existence by the word of God. They did not exist until the word of God was spoken. He said, *let there be light*, and light appeared. God wants us to understand when He speaks, it is done.

Scoffers are willingly ignorant. They have the mentality of the anti-Christ spirit which comes from Satan. The devil wants God's soldiers to doubt what God promised. He wants to shake our faith. We must understand our faith is our substance. It is our title deed. It is what proves to us that we have what God promised us. It is our tangible evidence or that which we hang onto. Our faith is what we cling to. If we do not have faith, we do not have anything tangible. We have nothing to hang onto.

BELIEF IN GOD'S WORD DETERMINES SOIL

If the scoffers can cause our faith to be shaken, we do not have any tangible evidence. Instead, we have doubt and unbelief. What will happen if we have no tangible evidence? It is quite simple. We are not going to receive the promise.

We must comprehend the scoffers, the ridiculers, the mockers are going to come. They can be our family, relatives, friends, associates, etc., but expect them to come. God says they will, and they will.

They question whether God really said it. *Hath God said? Are you sure it was God?* Whatever they can do to plant a seed of doubt. If we allow it to be sown, we start listening to them. They try to shake our faith. But God's soldiers must realize that between seedtime and harvest there will be storms, obstacles, strategies of Satan, trials, tribulations, scoffers, etc.

God is able to take those things which are not and make them as though they were. That is what faith is. It is able to take those things that are not, those things which we do not see in the natural, and see them by faith.

We believe because we know God has already brought them into existence. Our promise is answered in heaven, it is done. Now, we have to wait for the manifestation here. God already did it. He did it back in eternity. All the promises God has given each one of us has already been done in heaven. Now, comes the storm, the scoffers to discourage us while we wait.

Let me explain something. Although the promise is already done and we are in God's will, there may be other people involved, circumstances, situations that have to be lined up. So, we must not stagger at the promise of God through unbelief. We are not to doubt. We cannot allow anyone, or anything to encourage doubt.

Our faith is our evidence. It is the substance we hold onto. God is not a man that He can lie. We must be steadfast in our trust. He promised it, and we must believe we have it. We cannot look at the storm trying to uproot our faith.

How many owning a home would throw away our title deed because someone told us we do not really own the house? Sounds quite ludicrous, right? Why do so many throw away a title deed to a promise because of the storm, obstacles, strategies of Satan, scoffers, etc.?

Let God be true, and every man (and devil) be a liar (Romans 3:4). If God promised, He will do it. Now, when the storm comes, and it will come as sure as the sun rising and setting each day, we are to stand by faith with our title deed in hand. It will be a fight against our flesh until the finish. As long as we hang on to our faith until the storm ends, we will come out with our promise.

> Ye are of God, little children, and have overcome them: because greater is he that is in you, than he that is in the world (1 John 4:4).

God is the omnipotent one. He is greater than any power that comes against us. The power that comes against us is a created power. At any time God can cause that power to cease. When the disciples were in the boat, Jesus spoke to the storm, and it ceased (Mark 4:39).

At this present time, some of us are in the boat and the storm is rocking it furiously. We feel it will flood. We must take our eyes off the situation. We must hold onto our title deed, our promise.

If the devil can get us to focus on the situation or storm, we keep our eyes on the temporal or natural. We must turn our attention to the supernatural which can only be seen through the eyes of faith.

We do not see the promise with our natural eyes. That is why we must hang onto our title deed. It is like Jacob wrestling with the angel of the Lord all night and would not let go until he was blessed (Genesis 32:24-26). We hang on because we know God, we know He cannot lie, and we know He is able to perform his promise.

Because we have assurance in the word of God, we have determined to believe God no matter what. We hang on to our title deed and no man, woman, child, nor demon in hell is going to take it from us.

We are not going to allow God's word to be sown by the wayside for the devil to steal it, on stony ground where persecution for the word can cause it to have no root in itself, or among the thorns where the cares of this world, the deceitfulness of riches, or the lusts of other things choke the word and it becomes unfruitful. We have

BELIEF IN GOD'S WORD DETERMINES SOIL

prepared our heart, so God's word is sown in good soil, and we do not stumble through unbelief, but stand in our whole armor, take on the evil day, and bring forth fruit some thirty-fold, some sixty, and some an hundred!

Chapter 6

God's Soldiers Are Upheld

The steps of a good man are ordered by the LORD: and he delighteth in his way. Though he fall, he shall not be utterly cast down: for the LORD upholdeth him with his hand. I have been young, and now am old; yet have I not seen the righteous forsaken, nor his seed begging bread (Psalms 37:23–25).

STEPS

When we think of steps, we as parents are reminded of the first steps of our children. How important and exciting they were to us. Yet, once they were walking on their own, we were not mindful of their steps anymore. However, our Heavenly Father is always mindful of each step we take. He is aware of the importance of our steps and the necessity for them to be guided by him.

Do we realize the importance of our steps when considering our faith journey? A journey is made up of single steps, and one false step could be fatal. One step in the dark carries us off firm footing into an open trap, down a bank, or we could step right off the edge. Our first step down a wrong road is the beginning of troublesome, and possibly dangerous wanderings. Our steps are of the utmost importance in our spiritual journey, and we must comprehend this truth if we are to overcome this life.

GOOD MAN

There is nothing in the Hebrew for "good" man in our scripture text in Psalms. *Geber* is the original Hebrew word, and it properly signifies a strong man, a conqueror, or a hero. It appears to be used here to reveal that even the most powerful, the most mighty, the most athletic, the most formidable must be supported by the Lord, otherwise our strength or courage will be of little consequence.

The seven sons of Sceva thought they could cast out evil spirits by adjuring them by Jesus whom Paul preached. The evil spirit said, "Jesus I know, and Paul I know, but who are you?" And the man, in whom the evil spirit was, leapt on them, overcame them, and prevailed against them, so that they fled out of the house naked and wounded (Acts 19:13–16).

Only Jesus and God's soldiers have authority over evil spirits. We can be the most proficient body builder and have the courage of Goliath. Neither physical strength nor courage, without Jesus, will be able to stand against the powers of Hell.

> We are more than conquerors through him that loved us (Romans 8:37).

The good man, the strong man, the conqueror, the hero is a conqueror through Christ. We can do all things through Christ who strengthens us (Philippians 4:13).

ORDERED BY THE LORD

The steps of the good man, the strong man, the conqueror, the hero are ordered, directed, or designed by the Lord. His steps are so ruled by the Lord as to attain the end and favorable results at which God ordained.

Seeds of Knowledge

Established is the proper meaning of the Hebrew word for ordered. It means not only directed, but made firm, planted evenly and safely. The steps of God's soldiers are strengthened, established, upheld, or made firm by the Lord so that we shall not stumble nor fall into mischief.

It is not the general superintendence of men's steps and goings by God which is spoken of here. It is the special strengthening and supporting of the steps of the good man, the pious man, the man walking according to God's will. This informs us the path in which God's soldier treads is under God's guidance, upheld by his power, and directed by his counsel.

God orders and establishes the details of those who are walking with him. Details are of the immense importance everywhere. Step by step is the law of all progress. We are what the details of our life are.

What does that mean? Let me explain. The details of my life reveal what I am. If my details are evil, then I am unrighteous. If my details are good, then I am righteous. If I take righteous steps, then I am progressing or walking into godliness. If I take unrighteous steps, then I am progressing or walking into ungodliness.

God has a plan for the life of each one of us. Therefore, if our steps are details, then it is important who is designing or ordering our steps. Our little daily duties appear to have so slight importance to each other. Yet each step is leading us somewhere.

God's soldiers must comprehend that if God is ordering our steps, we should not be taking random, haphazard, or undesigned steps. We should not willingly move a step without his direction.

Okay, if our steps are designed or ordered by God, how can we take random or undesigned steps? It's quite simple. A free will may choose to obey another will. We can choose to walk our own way following our will, to do our own thing, or do whatever is comfortable on our flesh.

Choosing to take God's steps is most often the difficult steps. Our flesh does not like to be squeezed into a narrow path. Our flesh gets claustrophobia. However, our spirit can only survive when our flesh gets claustrophobia, is squeezed, or is dead to self.

Any time we yield to our flesh, we will obey the old nature, the adamic nature, the sinful nature. Whereas, our spirit wants to do the will of the new nature, the Christlike nature, the sinless nature. The best way to explain it is that once we are born again, we have two natures residing within.

To explain, I like to use the analogy of Dr. Jekyll and Mr. Hyde that portrays the battle quite efficiently. Mr. Hyde symbolizes our fleshly monster. Dr. Jekyll implies the spirit of God. It was a battle for Dr. Jekyll to keep Mr. Hyde under control.

In order to walk according the steps God has ordered, we must keep under our flesh, we must crucify our flesh, we must deny self, we must take up our cross daily, and follow Jesus. We must allow him to increase and continuously keep our flesh decreasing (John 3:30). We must decide or choose to walk contrary or opposite to the lust of the flesh, the lust of the eyes, the pride of life, and the flow of this life.

AND HE DELIGHTETH IN HIS WAY

If we delight, we are pleased with, we have pleasure, or we are content. When our steps (the good man, the pious man, the righteous man, the strong man, or the conqueror in Christ) are ordered by the Lord, we delight in our way, because it is that which God's Spirit has directed us. In other words, we delight in God's way and in the law and testimonies of our Maker.

> He is the Rock, his work is perfect: for all his ways are judgment: a God of truth and without iniquity, just and right is he (Deuteronomy 32:4).

God's soldiers delight in our way, because we know God is our Rock—the essence of stability and reliability. Because we know God is a God of truth and without iniquity, we know He will never direct a way that will lead to sin or in a way to lie. God will never lead us into anything that could be detrimental to our salvation or contrary to God's nature.

Seeds of Knowledge

Let no man say when he is tempted, I am tempted of God: for God cannot be tempted with evil, neither tempteth he any man: But every man is tempted, when he is drawn away of his own lust, and enticed (James 1:13-14).

God will never lead us into sin or that which is perilous to our spiritual life. He will always lead, direct, design our steps into righteousness.

We delight in our way because we know God will never change (Malachi 3:6), for He is the same yesterday, today, and forever (Hebrews 13:8). If God has promised mercy to the repented, then mercy is what the repentant will receive. Why? Because we are now walking in the way God ordered, the way God desires.

Why do God's soldiers delight in our way, even if it seems difficult? It is because we know that it has been ordered, ordained, directed by God. It is because we have learned as the Apostle Paul: *Not that I speak in respect of want: For I have learned, in whatsoever state I am, therewith to be content* (Philippians 4:11).

Our flesh may want things different, but we have decided to deny self what it wants. Because we know that we are in God's will, we CHOOSE to be content. We either decide to be content or complain in God's will. How we respond is determined upon the ground the seed of knowledge, the promise of God, or a revelation is sown. The soil is not prepared by the seed, but by our response or the condition of our heart to whatever seed God plants.

THOUGH HE FALL, HE SHALL NOT BE UTTERLY CAST DOWN BECAUSE THE LORD UPHOLDETH HIM WITH HIS HAND

The important fact here is that neither the text nor any of the versions insinuate, suggest, or imply that a falling into sin is meant in this verse. It implies a falling into trouble, distress, financial difficulty, sickness, adversity, misfortune, etc.

It has already been made clear if God is leading us, He will never direct us into sin. He cannot direct into that which is contrary to his nature. We may be cast down, overcome, overthrown by sickness, trouble, affliction, difficulty, poverty, enemies, etc., but we will not be totally or irrecoverably ruined. It will be remedied or changed. Why? Because the Lord sustains us (the good man) who are walking in the way He has ordered, and we are being held up by his hand.

> For without faith it is impossible to please him: for he that cometh to God must believe that he is, and that he is a rewarder of them that diligently seek him (Hebrews 11:6).

God's soldiers live that scripture. We know God will reward our diligent service to him. We know He will hold us up no matter what we may have to endure. We know sometimes our life will seem like all Hell has come against us. We know sometimes darkness will surround us like a heavy shroud. We know sometimes grief will seem unbearable.

> I will never leave thee nor forsake thee (Hebrews 13:5).

We may, for a season, FALL under the power of our adversaries, fall into distress, trouble, grief, sickness, financial difficulty, etc. Our life may challenge us with storms, obstacles, strategies of Satan, but the hand of God will ALWAYS be there to sustain us in whatever we face in life.

> The righteous cry, and the LORD heareth, and delivereth them out of all their troubles (Psalm 34:17).

At times, we would like to escape troubles or even the daily frustrations that continuously weigh us down, but God promises to help us to overcome them. He helps us to rise above the situation, by taking hold of our hand and lifting us up. In other words, there are times God is carrying us to help us get through the darkness.

A perfect example of our steps being ordered by the Lord and falling into distress is seen in Matthew 14:28-31. In these verses, Jesus bids Peter to walk on the water. Peter obeys, steps out of the ship, and walks on the water. However when he saw the storm, he was afraid, and began to sink. But when he cried out to Jesus to save him, Jesus immediately stretched forth his hand and caught him.

Before the adversity or peril could destroy Peter (before he could sink), the Lord reached out and upheld him by his hand. What is this revealing to us? It shows us that when we are walking in the steps ordered by God, we will FALL into adversity, hardships, difficulties, misfortune, and even danger. However, God will not allow it to utterly destroy us.

Someone falling into distress and darkness that was so overwhelming that He sweat drops of blood was Jesus (Luke 22:44). The crucifixion was the steps ordered by God. Jesus had to deny his flesh that didn't want to be separated from his Father for the first time in eternity. Yet, despite the battle, Jesus counted it joy (He had pleasure being in God's will to become our sin offering) and endured the cross for us (Hebrews 12:2).

Christ fell into trouble or distress to go to Calvary. The cross was the steps ordered or ordained by God. If Christ was to remain in his foreordained steps, He must go to Calvary and suffer that cruel death for us. Because He willingly walked in those steps, God upheld him to accomplish the path He had to walk.

British Pastor Alan Redpath said, "There is no circumstance, no trouble, no testing, that can ever touch me until, first of all, it has gone past God and past Christ, right through to me. If it has come that far, it has come with great purpose." If we realize that our steps include circumstances, troubles, testing that have been allowed by God for his great purpose, we, like Christ, will have joy knowing we are in God's will.

Why do we complain when God's will or his ordered steps become arduous upon our flesh? It's because our soil is not good ground. We either refuse to hear or obey it, allow persecution to discourage us, or become overwhelmed by the cares of this world, the deceitfulness of riches, or the lusts of other things.

Only as we become aware of God, his word, and the importance of walking in his ordered steps will we be enabled to prepare our hearts or our ground to be good soil. When we look upon our steps with pleasure because we know it is the plan of God for our life, we know we will not be destroyed because God upholds us with his hand. Such knowledge brings forth a harvest some thirty-fold, some sixty, and some an hundred!

Chapter 7

Good Soil Brings Forth His Craftsmanship

For by grace are ye saved through faith; and that not of yourselves: it is the gift of God: Not of works, lest any man should boast. For we are his workmanship, created in Christ Jesus unto good works, which God hath before ordained that we should walk in them (Ephesians 2:8–10).

CRAFTSMANSHIP IS THE QUALITY that comes from creating with passion, care, and attention to detail. It is a quality that is honed, refined.

When we are called God's workmanship, that is what is meant. We are God's craftsmanship created with passion, care, and attention to detail. He has honed (prepared) and refined (perfected) us through his refiner's fire to make us vessels of honor. God's soldiers were created to perform his good works that He ordained us to walk in before the foundation of the world.

All God's works, whatever they may be, are designed with the sole purpose of praising him. All that He does is done to point back to him. God is to be the only one who receives or gets glory for what He has done.

> I am the Lord: that is my name: and my glory will I not give to another, neither my praise to graven images (Isaiah 42:8).

The word glory in Isaiah means splendor, weight, or honor. God will not give the praise and honor due him to angels, demons, men, or idols. We must not take any glory for ideas, doctrines, works, wisdom, power, or ability that has come from God for his glory.

> For who maketh thee to differ from another? and what hast thou that thou didst not receive? now if thou didst receive it, why dost thou glory, as if thou hadst not received it? (1 Corinthians 4:7)

We think and reason because God has given us the ability to do so. If we receive wisdom, it is given by God. If we have received a great revelation, the Holy Spirit illuminated it. Whatever we know or whatever we accomplish, the ability has come from God. Everything we receive is a gift or talent from God, and we have nothing to boast about.

There is only one who has the right to boast or receive honor, fame, praise on his merit or his own accomplishments and that is God. Glory is that fame, honor, praise, etc. that is bestowed or attributed to the triumphs or work done. Think about it, has any person of his own merit earned the right to boast or claim glory on his achievements or feats?

Since God created us and endowed us with certain abilities, our only glorying should be in him. This is my seventeenth book (tenth nonfiction book on faith, the other seven are Christian fiction). Yet, I know to whom I owe the praise, glory, honor, and thanksgiving to. It is God who has given me the ability, talent, or gift to accomplish each feat. I am his craftsmanship. I am the work of his hands. Thus, whatever I achieve is to his glory.

Whatever He accomplishes, is to his glory. God is not the craftsmanship or the work of any hands. He is the Creator of all things. With that in mind, let's look at his works and see how they bring forth his glory.

> Mine hand also hath laid the foundation of the earth, and my right hand hath spanned the heavens; when I call unto them, they stand up together (Isaiah 48:13).

God laid the foundation of the earth and spanned the heavens with his right hand. How can man think to bring down the Almighty who measured the heavens with his right hand or the length between the tip of a thumb and little finger? God is so vast that our finite minds cannot fathom his immensity. He is beyond our comprehension. Who can we liken God to? Who can we compare him with?

Our salvation reveals the glory of God. His grace or free unmerited love and favor has enabled us to receive mercy, pardon, and privilege. We have done nothing to deserve such a privilege. It is all on the part of God, and all his merit. We can claim no ability to save ourselves. The grace or the influence of God on our heart is the only reason our hearts are renewed. In ourselves, our own merit, we could not save ourselves or keep ourselves from sin.

> As it is written, There is none righteous, no, not one: There is none that understandeth, there is none that seeketh after God. They are all gone out of the way, they are together become unprofitable; there is none that doeth good, no, not one (Romans 3:10–12).

If God, in his love, mercy, and grace, did not come after us like a man trying to win his bride, we would still be gone out of the way. We would never on our own seek after God. We would never understand the love of God. We would continue to do nothing good in the eyes of God.

It is not in the human nature to have faith in God. His grace, his salvation, and even faith is bestowed from God. Our salvation, our faith, and God's grace are all his gift to us when we repent of our sins and accept Christ's redemptive work on the cross.

If faith was on our part, it would be our work or our merit. But salvation, grace, faith are not by works. They are God's gifts, or we would boast that we had part in our salvation. Since it all comes from God or is God's gift, then the boast is him and the glory is his and his alone.

Salvation must be either of grace or works; the two cannot be mixed together. If it be works in any degree, it is no more grace. If it was works in any degree, it would afford or give us occasion to boast. Then it would be a debt paid and not a gift bestowed.

The plan of salvation is altogether of grace from first to last. The Savior who wrought it out for us, the acceptance of his vicarious sacrifice, and the faith whereby we are made partakers of his sacrifice are all the gifts of God's free and sovereign grace.

Once we comprehend the greatness of God's love and grace, we understand how much we owe him. It is an enormous debt, and we can never repay a microscopic part of it. This helps us to realize what being his craftsmanship is.

There is a difference between our works and being his craftsmanship created in Christ Jesus unto good works. God has given to us a new nature and infused our souls with a new and heavenly principle.

Under the influence of the Holy Spirit, we move in a new direction, concerning the things of the Spirit, whereas, before we were concerned about the things of the flesh. Now, the new creation is his work or his craftsmanship. When our works are the result of his working in us, it is no longer we that liveth but Christ that liveth in us (Galatians 2:20).

Our good works, when we behold his salvation, love, mercy, and grace, are an obligation, debt, duty that we owe. How can we behold what He has done and not feel obligated to him? How can we claim to be his, be a recipient of his grace and have little or no desire to please him?

Good works are doing whatever we can to please God. Pleasing God and doing what we can for the Body of Christ is the only path in which it is possible for us to arrive at our Father's house. How can we willfully turn aside from it?

If we are his creation, his workmanship or craftsmanship, our works will show it is him working through us and not us. It is by our works that men judge our principles. Our principles are our motives, our cause of action, what is behind what we do, our objectives, our intentions, etc.

When our life is the result of God working through us:

1. We will be Christlike in this world.
2. We will confess Christ before all men.
3. We will take on the evil day in his full armor.
4. We will not seek after accolades of men.
5. We will deny self, take up our cross daily, and follow Jesus.
6. We will be known as followers of Christ by our life.
7. We will love God above everyone and anything.
8. We will strive to be holy as He is holy.
9. We will have the seed of knowledge sown on good ground.

If we frustrate the grace of God and not allow him to work those good works, we will put a stumbling block in the way of others and cause them to fall. It is God's soldiers who, by our good works, that are to light up or clear the way for others to find their way to Christ. Are we a light in this dark world? If we are not, then we are a stumbling block to our family, friends, etc.

When we become the craftsmanship of God created in Christ our works give glory to God. They glorify God because our works become good works, not in man's meaning of good, but God's definition of good. Our works are godly, righteous, merciful. They are him extending his love, mercy, grace, etc. through us.

Even being his craftsmanship created in Christ unto good works is his gift. As we can refuse his gift of love, his gift of salvation, etc., we can refuse to be his craftsmanship of good works. We can refuse to be the vessel He does good or righteous, merciful, helpful, etc. works through. If we remember that we are not our own, but we were bought with the price of Christ's blood, we would submit to being his craftsmanship.

If we receive his gift of grace for salvation, it must include his gift of being his craftsmanship. He did not offer us the gift of his grace unto salvation and end it there in a place of selfishness. But He offered it that, upon our acceptance of it, we live for him and others.

God did not save us for our own satisfaction, gratification, pleasure, enjoyment. If we were, we would have no more need to still be here. However, we are not saved for our own fulfillment, but to be used as God's craftsmanship to touch the lives of others in whatever way He has given us the gifts, talents, and ability to do. He is only glorified in the life that shows forth his virtues. The true creation or craftsmanship of God shows Christ not self.

In chapter three, I mentioned what the Apostle Paul suffered for the love of Christ. He suffered all he did because he chose to be God's craftsmanship. He was willing to suffer persecution, affliction, distress, anguish, loneliness, etc. to bring God's love, mercy, grace to others.

How many of God's soldiers are willing to be God's craftsmanship? How many are willing to suffer for the cross of Christ? How many are willing to deny self for the glory of God? How many are willing to give up our life and allow Christ to live through us?

> This know also, that in the last days perilous times shall come. For men shall be lovers of their own selves, covetous, boasters, proud, blasphemers, disobedient to parents, unthankful, unholy, With natural affection, trucebreakers, false accusers, incontinent (lack of self-restraint), fierce, despisers of those that are good, Traitors, heady, highminded, lovers of pleasures more than lovers of God (2 Timothy 3:1–4).

> Woe unto them that call evil good, and good evil; that put darkness for light, and light for darkness; that put bitter for sweet, and sweet for bitter! (Isaiah 5:20)

We are living in these days of perilous, dangerous, hazardous, unsafe times. All we have to do is see the news and know that self-love is prevalent. Anarchy (chaos, lawlessness, rebellion, riots) is seen as good and the rule of law is seen as evil. Christians are considered evil, and socialism, Marxism, communism, etc. are considered good. Trying to defund the police, who are our wall of protection against the anarchy rising in this country, reveals the perilous times are upon us.

As we observe the list of effects taking place in the last days, we conclude that "lovers of self" directs the rest of the list. Only as we become a self-lover will we be covetous, boasters, proud, unholy, etc.

This list could generate fear in God's craftsmanship if we do not understand God's love. The Apostle Paul was well aware of these

GOOD SOIL BRINGS FORTH HIS CRAFTSMANSHIP

sort of individuals and knew how to overcome whoever or whatever challenged his faith in Christ because he was rooted in the love of God.

Without being in the inner veil and experiencing God's love, we will not withstand the perilous or dangerous times that are becoming more prevalent. We must so trust his love that we can withstand persecution, affliction, adversity, storms, obstacles, strategies of Satan without fear of what man can do unto us.

God's soldiers must rise up in the full armor of God and stand against the evil permeating our homes, our schools, our places of employment, our government, our families, etc. and proclaim the Gospel of Christ to this lost and dying world. Soldiers of God, if we don't stand against the destruction that is coming into our country, who else will?

God promises if his people who are called by his name, shall humble themselves, and pray, and seek my face, and turn from their wicked ways; then will I hear from heaven, and will forgive their sin, and will heal their land (2 Chronicles 7:14).

Our Nation has sinned against God. Why do I say that? Look at what we have allowed to take place in our country.

1. We have allowed prayer to be taken out of our schools.
2. We have taken the ten Commandments out of public buildings.
3. We have legalized abortion (the murder of unborn and born children).
4. We have legalized homosexual marriage which is an abomination to God.
5. We have legalized marijuana (a psychoactive drug that changes brain function and results in alterations in perception, mood, consciousness, cognition, or behavior).
6. We have allowed those who refuse to be sworn in on the Bible to hold positions in our Government, when this is a Christian Nation founded upon the Judeo-Christian belief system.
7. We overlook sins that will not inherit the kingdom of God like fornication, adultery, effeminate (homosexuals), drunkards, etc. (1 Corinthians 6:9–10).

8. We have given children rule over parents, for parents are afraid to correct their children because of governmental interference.

Christianity has become so desensitized to the truth of God's word that it believes sin is a sickness. It believes that it is a woman's right to have an abortion (to murder her child) because it would be inconvenient to have the baby. It believes that homosexuality is an alternate lifestyle. It believes that a man was born in a woman's body or a woman was born in man's body. Many no longer base their beliefs on the truth of scripture, but on man's opinion, science, or whatever is contrary to God's word.

How has this come about in our Nation? It is quite simple when we comprehend the soil upon which God's seed of knowledge, promise, or revelation is sown.

1. How many of God's soldiers have rejected or resisted the word because it didn't rest well with our flesh and allowed the seed to fall by the WAYSIDE?
2. How many of God's soldiers deny Christ daily because we do not stand up for him or his word to avoid persecution and allow the seed to fall on STONY GROUND?
3. How many of God's soldiers are selling our birthright for a temporary fleshly indulgence because of the *cares of this life*? How many of God's soldiers are coveting more money at the neglect of our relationship with God because of the *deceitfulness of riches*? How many of God's soldiers allow the desire or lust after man's approval to cause us to be closet Christians because we allow the *lusts of approval* (lusts of other things)? All these are seeds sown among the THORNS that will choke the seed of knowledge, promise, or revelation.

Christianity is bowing down to other gods of compromise, self-indulgence, pursuit of riches, man's approval, scientific knowledge, etc. God is no longer our God, but whatever pleases the flesh, that we are supposed to deny, has become god.

Psalm 33:12 says, "Blessed is the nation whose God is the Lord (Jehovah)." How can God bless our nation when much of Christianity serves other gods to satisfy our lust of the flesh, our lust of the eyes, and our pride of life? Much of Christianity is not the craftsmanship of God and are not accomplishing his will in our lives, our home, our workplace, our schools, our church, our government, our country.

The soil upon which the seed of knowledge is sown determines the harvest of the seed. It's time for God's soldiers to carefully contemplate our lives. Are we living for Christ or self? Are we allowing the Holy Spirit conviction to turn us from sin? Are we a light in this dark world leading others to Christ? Are we suffering persecution, affliction, adversity, troubles through sharing the gospel message to others or are we denying him to avoid any conflict?

What is the condition of our heart or the soil upon which the seed of knowledge, promise, or revelation is sown? Are we listening to teachers with itching ears that allow us to believe we are serving Christ while living in sin? Have we allowed our ears to become dull of hearing because our flesh is uncomfortable adhering to the scriptures? Are we more concerned about pleasure in this life than denying self? Have we convinced ourselves that the sins that will not inherit the kingdom of God does not mean us because we said a sinner's prayer? Have we separated ourselves from this world and cleaved onto God?

What God's soldiers need to ponder is who has priority, precedence, importance in our life, who or what do we love more than anything or anyone. Who is our life? Is it Christ or self? The answer to that question determines whether the seed of knowledge, promise, or revelation is sown by the wayside, on stony ground, among the thorns, or on good ground.

If Christ is our life or our everything, the seed of knowledge is sown on good ground, gives glory to God alone, and brings forth a harvest of fruit some thirty-fold, some sixty, and some an hundred!

www.ingramcontent.com/pod-product-compliance
Lightning Source LLC
Chambersburg PA
CBHW071748040426
42446CB00012B/2495